Praise for Hairy and Hopper to the Rescue

- Any child who has struggled to learn will be encouraged by this story. Linda Jessup recreates her nine-year-old self with warmth and wit, remembering how she "discovered her brain" during a time when school was difficult and her usual friends, and even her siblings, weren't allowed to see her. Linda helps us to understand that it's not what happens to you; it's what you do about it. Everyone should have a "Linda" in their lives.
  Betty Lou Bettner, author of *The Creative Force* and *Raising Kids Who Can*

- Linda Jessup captivated our Rotary district conference by telling her story of what it was like to have polio. She helped renew our commitment to Rotary International's program to eradicate this dreaded virus once and for all. Her delightful book serves another of our programs: increasing literacy among grade-school children through the art of storytelling. We plan to tell her story widely through local school districts.
  Philip Murphy, Past Rotary District 5440 Governor and Spellbinder Storyteller

- The covid pandemic isn't the first disease to leave children isolated and alone, separated from school, friends and family. The current crop of grade-schoolers will identify with Linda's struggle with polio and post-polio while learning about a virus that has been absent from the U.S. for nearly thirty years, but still lurks in several countries, awaiting a chance to spread once again. This is a well-written story of the author's mental and physical efforts to live life despite adversity with a lifelong illness.
  Dr. Robert Tello, MD, BCIM, CMD

Hairy and Hopper to the Rescue

The true story of a very sick girl and her *extremely* unusual friends.

Linda E. Jessup

Illustrated by Yohanna Roe Jessup

Harry and Hopper to the Rescue

ISBN 978-0-578-90580-8
Promise Press

Dedication

To polio survivors everywhere, and to the members of
Rotary International who have dedicated their time,
resources and sometimes their lives to polio's eradication

Acknowledgments

Thanks to the Rotarians in Colorado and Maryland who invited me to read earlier versions of this story to their chapter and district meetings and who provided valuable feedback and encouragement for publishing it.

To my daughter Yohanna Jessup for her creativity and artistry in capturing my story in beautiful illustrations.

And to David M. Jessup, my husband of fifty-five years and author of three historical novels, who helped critique my drafts and guided the book through publication.

Australia, 1950

"I'm sick," I told my mother. "And I'm dizzy. I hurt all over my body."

It was a school day in the tropical early spring of 1950. I was a 9-year-old girl, living "down under," as people in Brisbane, Australia, say, with my parents and three sisters. Usually I was a regular healthy kid, full of energy and mischief. But on this day I woke up with a blasting headache that ran like lightning fire down my neck, back and into my arms and legs.

Mother turned from setting out breakfast and looked at me--hard. She felt my forehead, looked down my throat and then shook her head firmly. "Oh no you don't, Linda," she said. "I'm not stupid. You've tried to fool me too often. Just last week it was the lipstick 'measles' that smeared the next day. *I'm the stupid one*, I thought. *Now Mother doesn't believe me anymore because I tried that dumb measles trick to get out of school.*

I dreaded school because I was what they called "a slow reader." Reading in front of the class was the worst. It made me feel totally stupid. I would get so nervous I could hardly breathe. All I wanted to do was to get outside to run around until I could calm down.

My three sisters were all super smart. Compared to them I was way behind. My oldest sister sometimes called me "Dim Bulb," like a light bulb about to go out. I didn't like it, but I didn't punch her or argue about it because I thought she was right. I figured if I had ever had brains, I had lost them somewhere along the way.

"But Mommy, this time I really *AM* sick," I pleaded, my voice coming out all shaky.

Mother was busy buttoning up my little sister's public-school uniform. "Well, you seem fine to me, Honey. I hate to have you miss more classes than you already have. But if something really *IS* wrong, the school will send you home."

So I set off on wobbly, aching legs, only to have my teacher, Mr. Onwin, call for the school nurse awhile later. The nurse did send me home, but for the first time ever I really *wasn't* glad to be sick.

The sun was so bright, I could hardly see. It hurt my eyes. Every *part* of me hurt. And I could only walk a few steps at a time before I had to sit down on the hot curb until I could get enough energy to stand up and take a few more shaky steps.

It took me a long time. When I finally got to our house, Mother took my temperature. She got very quiet, but this time not mad quiet. She said, like she was

talking to herself, "I've *never* seen a temperature so high! This is over 104 degrees!" Gently she carried me to the guest bedroom, across from her and Daddy's room.

As in all our bedrooms, mosquito netting hung on a wooden frame over the whole bed and all the way to the

floor. Those white folds of netting were the last thing I remember.

I was wakened from a deep sleep by my mother and a man in a white coat. He was trying to pull me up in bed. He said, "Linda, I'm Dr. Nye. Listen to me, this is important. I need you to sit up and bend both of your knees, like a tent." He pulled me up into position and I almost screamed from the pain. "Now lean forward and touch your forehead to your knees."

I struggled to follow his directions so he wouldn't pull on me again. But I felt limp, confused. The pain was so strong I couldn't do it. Dr. Nye gave my head a little push forward. It hurt so much, I fainted.

A few days later as I fought to come out of a murky, pain-filled haze, Mother slid her arm behind my shoulders and tried to spoon water into my mouth. "Welcome back, Honey," she said, relief in her voice. "You've been delirious."

I tried to think what "delirious" meant as I swallowed spoonsful of water-- once, twice, three times.

"I've been sponging you off with cool water for two days to get your fever down. I'm glad you can drink a little bit now, so you won't have to go to the hospital. Dr. Nye says you have Polio Flu. He comes by every day to check on you. Here." She offered me the glass.

I thought I was reaching for the water, but my right arm and hand didn't move. I couldn't feel anything but hurt over my whole body. I tried to reach again. Nothing. Something was terribly wrong.

Mother looked very serious now. She propped me up on pillows. "Can you move your legs?"

I tried to lift each one, but only the right leg trembled a little bit. Everything ached. It was too much. I felt myself slipping away, exhausted, back into the black hole of sleep.

My new world became very small over the next two months. Only Mother and Dr. Nye could come in my room. A big white bucket of Clorox water sat by the

door. Anything that touched me—including the rubber gloves Mother wore--had to be soaked in that bucket.

I found out later the Health Department had put up a big sign on our fence. The sign said, "Quarantine." That meant that no one except our family and the doctor could enter our yard or house.

Mother came in twice a day with a big tub of steaming hot wool cloths cut out of Daddy's old coat. She wrapped these hot strips around my arms and legs before helping me do exercises. The cloths stank and burned at first, but I quickly learned not to cry. Crying just made us both sad, and it wore me out.

When the hot wool cooled a little, my muscles didn't ache so much, and the exercises went better too. But I was always sore, and my arms and legs were bright red from first degree burns, and so were Mother's hands,

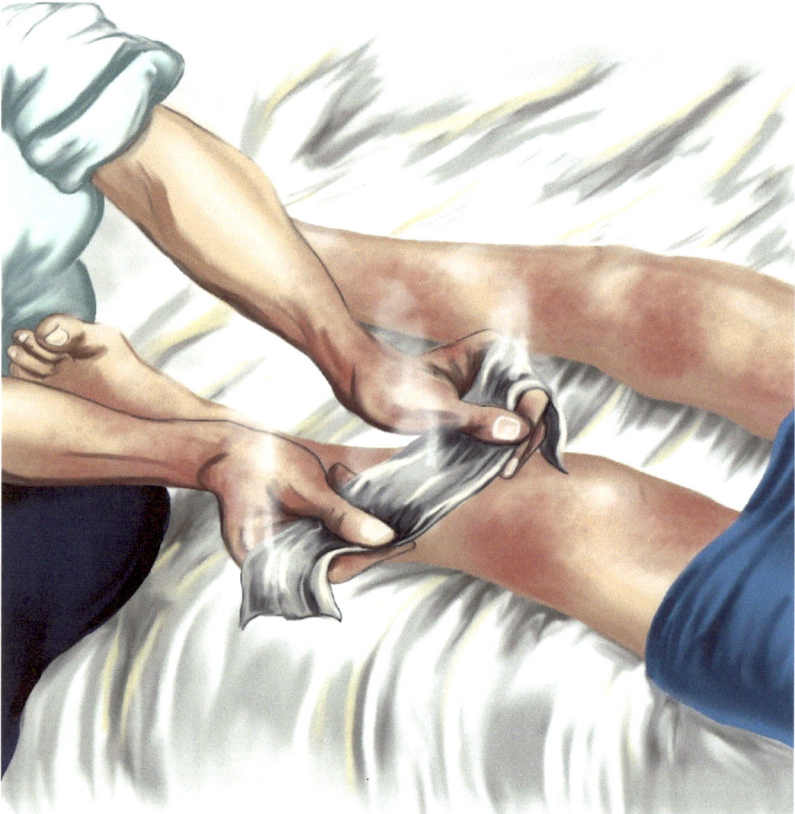

and wrists.

Mother said her "sister Kenny" recommended this treatment. I thought "Kenny" was a boys' name, and I thought Mother's only little sister had died soon after she was born. But thinking was so tiring I couldn't remember to ask about it. Later I found out that Sister Kenny was a famous Australian nurse who figured out the best way to help people with polio was with wet heat and muscle exercises, instead of putting them in hard casts or splints where their muscles just got weaker and shriveled up.

As I began to get better, I spent most of every day alone, looking at the wavy cream and light blue paint on the ceiling. At first my sisters made cards and pictures for me and called to me as they left for school. But as hard as I tried, my voice was so weak they couldn't hear me. After a while they stopped trying. I could still hear them, talking, laughing, yelling, and sometimes arguing in the house or yard. But I decided they had probably forgotten about me by then.

One day as Mother was unrolling the first of the hot cloths, I asked if Rosalee, my best friend and playmate from across the street, could come over and talk to me. She could stand right outside the narrow window on the other side of the double bed. Mother didn't answer for a moment. Then she came over, sat down on my bed and stroked my head. Finally she said "Don't you remember Linda? Rosalee's in the hospital. She has the really bad kind of polio." I remember thinking, "*Well I guess I'm lucky then. I must have the really <u>good</u> kind of polio.*"

I never saw or heard anything about Rosalee again. Then her family moved away.

Very slowly, as the weeks, and then four months went by, I started feeling better. My fever disappeared, but the aching in my back, neck, legs and arm muscles continued. The better I got, the more I missed my sisters and schoolmates. I also felt very bored.

When my left hand grew strong enough to hold onto a magazine and I was able to sit up for a while, propped up by pillows, Mother brought me a copy of Cricket Magazine. With nothing else to do, I began trying to sound out words in the magazine and figure out their meaning by looking at the pictures and drawings. Some were poems. The rhymes also helped me figure out the right words. Little by little, as my left hand slowly started to come back alive, some of those words and their meanings started to come alive for me too.

Then one day Mother brought me a book named A *Child's Garden of Verses*. For days I didn't touch that big book, thinking it would be too hard to read. When I finally opened it, I found *it* had good pictures too, including some of animals. I loved animals, especially horses! Before getting polio flu I spent most of my time outdoors, running, climbing trees, and exploring nature. So I began trying to sound out some of the words in the shortest poems, especially the ones that had pictures of animals on the pages.

I discovered I could remember my favorite poems, word-for-word. I called it "rememberizing." Mother helped me with any words I just couldn't get by myself when she came with the hot cloths. Sometimes I said the good poems out loud in my whispery voice. I loved the sound of the rhymes, the rhythm of the words, the pictures and stories the poems painted in my imagination.

Then, one long hot, afternoon, I decided to surprise my mother by "rememberizing" the entire poem of "Horton Hatches the Egg," by Dr. Seuss, which was printed in one of the Cricket magazines. I was looking at the ceiling, reciting one of the many verses, when I noticed the mosquito netting on the far side of my bed shaking-- *hard*. I wondered. *Is this what people call an 'earthquake'?* I dropped the magazine and watched.

Suddenly three long hairy legs -- striped black and tan-- appeared on top of the netting over the far edge of the bed, followed by a head with two fuzzy tusks, a dark brown furry body and five more striped legs.

The monster thing was a spider, a tarantula, I guessed, bigger than my little sister's whole hand! It came quickly across the mosquito net straight toward me. I desperately tried to remember if tarantulas bite. If they attacked people and killed them, or if they spit poison. I pressed myself as far back in the pillows as I could, hugely grateful for the six-or-so inches of space between my face, and the netting keeping the spider out. I tried to call for Mother, but only squeaky sounds came out, like a sheep bleating. No words.

The huge tarantula and I stared at each other. It had glittery black eyes—cold, cruel eyes, I thought--about the size of large pinheads. I wished Mother would come, even with the hot stinky cloths. But the house was silent. After a *very* long time the spider wriggled its fuzzy tusks, turned, and crawled back across the bed, the way it had come. Whew! I stopped pressing back on the pillows and began panting. I guess I had been holding my breath.

At first, I felt desperate to tell Mother about the tarantula. But when she did finally come, for some reason, I didn't say anything. She was hurrying, and cranked open the window while she waited for the hot cloths to relax my muscles. "It's awfully stuffy in here," she said, wiping her forehead with her reddened wrist. I could hear my sisters laughing as they made snacks in the kitchen.

That same evening, I had my second visitor. A small, green frog, jumped up onto the low window sill. The frog seemed to watch me with one eye. But every once in a while, its rosy tongue zipped out, so fast I could hardly see it, to catch a moth, mosquito, or beetle. I

thought to myself, "Wow! Two visitors, who were not afraid of me, in one day!"

From that day on, I felt less lonely. The tarantula appeared almost every afternoon. I began to look forward to seeing the netting shake and his black and brown body pop over the far edge of my bed. I liked watching him crawl gracefully across the netting with his long hairy legs, and stop, a few inches from my face. I had named the frog "Hopper", so I named the tarantula too. I called him "Hairy." He no longer scared me. In fact he began to look a lot like every other curious, furry animal I had ever seen.

One long, hot afternoon, I noticed that Harry's round black eyes were glistening, sort of teary looking instead of fierce. He looked …sad. I asked, "Are you lonely, Hairy?" Without thinking, I reached out with my right pointer finger and stroked his furry tummy. Hairy crouched against the netting, like a dog getting its stomach rubbed. When I stopped, he stood straight. When I touched him again, he crouched down for more scratching.

After that day I always talked to Hairy and he seemed to like to listen. I looked for poems to recite to him, especially those with spiders or bugs in them. I also talked and read to Hopper, my frog friend, on the evenings he showed up. I practiced reading them *Horton Hatches the Egg* until I'd completely "rememberized" it by heart. I liked to pretend that *I* was their teacher and *they* were my students!

By this time, five months had gone by. I was getting stronger by the day and could sit up against the pillows on my own. Sitting up made me taller than Harry, but he didn't seem afraid. I could also begin to move my left leg around, though it was still pretty shaky and very skinny. My body didn't hurt as much or feel tired all the time, either. I was getting restless. Tired of being in bed. So I decided to train my thin leg to walk again.

How to practice walking? This was a tricky question. My right leg was pretty weak after not being used much, though Mother still did my hot packs and arm and leg exercises twice every day. I started practicing in my room, at night, standing on each leg in turn and leaning my body on the bed. After a while, I began standing, barefoot, hopping on my right foot when the left got wobbly and started to ache. One night I decided I needed more space to practice. I waited until everyone was asleep. Then I went quietly hopping out through the dark house, like Hopper the frog. After that I practiced almost every night.

One afternoon, when I had finished reciting *Horton* by heart for Harry and was feeling almost normal again, some surprising thoughts suddenly came to me. A lot had happened since I had gotten sick with Polio Flu six months ago. I had learned to read out loud without stumbling or giving up. And without feeling nervous or stupid I had figured out how to "rememberize" a lot of poems. I had taught myself how to hop around at night and even walk a little and make my legs stronger, without anybody knowing. I could recite the entire story of "Horton Hatches the Egg" by heart, and lots of other poems too. I had learned to be patient and I had tamed two wild animals. I couldn't be too stupid!

Then it hit me! Out of all those months of sickness and loneliness, something amazing had happened. It wasn't fast. It wasn't easy. And I still wasn't as smart as my clever sisters. But at long last, when I least expected it, I had found my brains! With the help of my two brave and faithful friends.

Afterward

Like many polio survivors, I fought hard to resume a "normal" life after my nine-year-old bout with the virus. I got rid of my hated braces, learned to walk without a limp, and returned with my family to Ogden, Utah, to resume school after losing one year of classes. We didn't talk about polio, which at the time was considered somehow shameful, as if contracting the virus was associated with deficient home conditions.

I dated boys in high school and college, worked at a high-altitude research station in Colorado, skied and hiked and rode horses, got married and raised three biological and four foster children, founded a parent education program and directed it for 25 years, and "retired" to an active life hosting guests at my husband's family's dude ranch in Colorado. That was in 2000. I was 60 years old, in fine health.

Or so I thought.

In Colorado I began noticing shortness of breath when I hiked up mountain trails I had previously climbed with ease. New aches and pains troubled my muscles. Sleep sometimes overtook me when I stopped for a red light in my car.

On a stormy afternoon during a cattle drive, as lightning and thunder lashed the darkness and wind, rain and hail hit full on, the herd spooked and ran over the rocky top of Eagle Ridge and down steep hillsides into the relative cover of wooded gulches. As nervous as I was about lightning, I felt even more shaken by my growing loss of balance and trouble keeping my seat in the saddle.

Something was very wrong and getting worse. I panted from the effort and nearly fell when I dismounted. My arms trembled, then ached for hours after I unsaddled. Internists, neurologists and pulmonologists could find no source for my symptoms. My medical history consisted only of polio, 55 years earlier at age 9.

One doctor said I should exercise more. Another said exercise less. I hemorrhaged after an unnecessary surgical cardiac evaluation. I was given oxygen, which turned my lips blue and caused mental confusion. A C-PAP respirator was prescribed, but it seemed to smother me.

Finally, after three years of searching for answers, I found one of a small handful of polio clinics in the country and was diagnosed with Post-Polio Syndrome. This is not a return of the polio virus. It is, I learned, a gradual weakening of ageing muscles due to nerve damage from viral action fifty years earlier.

My pride in overcoming polio was dealt a blow. I had to use a Bi-PAP respirator to keep my polio-weakened diaphragm breathing at night. Eventually I had to leave Colorado and return to our home in Maryland in order to avoid carrying oxygen tanks at Colorado altitudes.

I learned about Rotary's campaign to eradicate polio in the world, starting with the March of Dimes during my childhood and continuing today with mass vaccination campaigns in the few countries where polio is still present.

In Colorado I joined Loveland Rotary and worked with the Rotary District Polio Committee to help finish the fight against polio. Finding myself physically unable to join immunization teams, I helped produce four videos, now on YouTube under *Faces of Polio in the USA*, and began giving talks to Rotary clubs to solicit donations, grants and encouragement to continue the fight against polio.

These videos are helping to educate American parents about the continuing need to vaccinate their children against polio, and other "old" diseases. They are informing doctors and other medical care providers about the existence of post-Polio Syndrome and some of the hazards and problems these polio survivors face. One video gives polio survivors with Post-Polio Syndrome a voice about what they wish their care providers knew.

Once the End Polio Now campaign has succeeded, survivors around the world will still be experiencing the life-changing fall-out of Post-Polio Syndrome for much of the next century. My hope is that these people will not be forgotten.

About the Author

Linda Jessup is Founder of the Parent Encouragement Program (PEP) an independent non-profit parent education center located in Kensington, Maryland.

During her more than thirty-five years of experience as a Family Nurse Practitioner, parent educator, radio talk show host, author and mother of seven children-- biological, foster and adoptive--she developed the curriculum that forms the core of her 2014 book, *Parenting with Courage and Uncommon Sense*, co-authored with Emory Luce Baldwin.

When Linda learned of Rotary's commitment to eradicating polio, she joined the Loveland, Colorado, Rotary club and co-chaired the Polio and Membership Committees.

She also served for years on the District Polio Committee, which produced four original YouTube videos about polio. The first was titled *Faces of Polio in the USA*. A second was about the rarely identified Post-Polio Syndrome. The third dealt with the urgent need to improve vaccination coverage, and the fourth identified what medical care providers need to know about Post-Polio Syndrome. These videos regularly receive hits from almost every country in the world.

Yohanna Roe Jessup creates inspirational drawings, paintings, and digital art. When she's not painting you can find her meditating or meandering on long hikes through California parks. www.yohannajessup.com

www.ingramcontent.com/pod-product-compliance
Lightning Source LLC
Chambersburg PA
CBHW041742040426
42443CB00004B/90